It's Not You,
It's Your Job Search

10 Ways Your Job Search is Messing With Your Mind

(Plus 43 Super-Practical Tips to Undo the Voodoo)

By Cliff Flamer

Haveline Publications

OAKLAND

HAVELINE PUBLICATIONS, March 2020
571 Mira Vista Avenue, Oakland, CA 94610

All inquiries should be made to the author:

Cliff Flamer
CEO, BrightSide Resumes
http://www.brightsideresumes.com

Front cover design by Dylan Glockler & Daniel Ojedokun.
Back cover design by Baltasar Gracian.
Copyediting by Camille Gregory & Michelle McGill.
Author Photo & Interior Photo Design by Dylan Glockler.

ISBN: 978-1-7347444-0-8

Printed in the United States of America.

TABLE OF CONTENTS

This book is dedicated to job seekers everywhere,

because looking for work is hard and every one of us needs

a little support to become who we're supposed to be.

INTRODUCTION

Some Empathy for the Job Seeker

Looking for work can be one of the loneliest, one-sided, labor-intensive, and fruitless activities we ever take on, even when we're doing everything right! The most accomplished among us spiral into a dizzying tailspin of Impostor Syndrome. Within just a few weeks of looking for work, we get tired, anxious, hopeless, bitter, lost, paralyzed, and depressed.

The good news is it's not you; it's the job search.

This book is 10 short chapters. Each describes an aspect of the job search that may be messing with your mind. Then, I follow it up with some practical strategies to get you back on track so you can be your best self during this pivotal time.

CHAPTER 1

Personal Branding
The Shortsightedness of Selling Yourself

I enjoy selling my music.

I don't enjoy selling myself.

JAMES TAYLOR

Everything out there about job-searching tells you to sell yourself, to accept that you're a product and the employer is the buyer. Indeed, the resume is often referred to as a marketing document, just as the elevator pitch has been recast as your personal brand.

This marketing metaphor is uncomfortable to wear. People aren't products. No one wants to see themselves as a shrink-wrapped widget. And here's the worst part: when you're selling something you don't believe in, you don't sell a whole lot of them!

If your job search isn't giving you much return, it's because you're stuck in selling mode. No one wants to be sold to. Do you know anyone who gets excited about walking into a car dealership? Or being accosted by a smarmy voice on a pop-up video?

You're not a product, and as long as you present like one, no one's going to walk onto your car lot or click on your "Buy Now" button.

Being inauthentic may turn some heads, but ultimately, it leads to being tired, bitter, and aloof, like a blow-hard salesman with a shtick that's not working. People can see right through it, and it's messing with your mind.

> **Don't sell yourself. *Show* yourself.**

A bit of a reframe is in order here. Instead of seeing a job search as selling yourself, think of it as an opportunity to discover what you're really about and hold that up for the world to see. Big difference. *Selling* yourself feels fake and drains you. *Showing* yourself feels authentic and energizes you. Indeed, it transforms you.

Whenever you're feeling lost or frustrated with your job search, stop looking out and instead, look inward. Forget about the people out there and get back to YOU. Answer a few of these questions and you'll find your compass: Which work activities cause you to lose track of time? What advice do people seek from you? What would your favorite colleague say is your superpower? What could you do all day? In these answers, you'll find the power of your story.

> **Test your story to remember your greatness.**

The good news is the things that make you great are intertwined throughout your entire life. Take any of these achievements you just came up with and reflect on earlier phases of your life. I'll bet you can find a similar story, both in work and in your personal life. I know this because I've been career coaching people for years and there is always a connection between past and present accomplishments. In order for you to tell a great story, you have to believe in your story first. And history is your crystal ball.

> Trade your elevator pitch for an IM Intro.

Yes, your spiel should be brief, but it shouldn't be corny or contrived. Speak as if you're writing a quick text to the employer to tell them who you are. To stay authentic, act as if you're communicating with a friend of a friend. In fact, to test your IM Intro, try it on a friend. If you can't do it without feeling uncomfortable or self-conscious, that means it's not ready yet. You should be able to introduce yourself in your own voice without the two of you busting out laughing. Keep it short, modest, and accessible. You're trying to start a conversation, not convince someone to drop everything and hire you on the spot.

> You are not a product.

Never try to be someone you're not. You can be compelling simply by telling people about the cool things you've done. Pick your greatest hits but allow yourself to be truthful and fallible. Get excited about your stories as they actually happened. Let your work speak for itself.

CHAPTER 2

Job Applications
Throwing Perfect Pitches into a Black Hole

The worst thing:

To give yourself away in exchange for not enough love.

JOYCE CAROL OATES

How Job Applications Are Messing with Your Mind

Imagine you're in the 9th inning of the World Series. You're throwing the absolute best pitches you've ever thrown—perfect strikes every time—but the umpire isn't calling them. Worse, the pitches seem to disappear as they cross the plate. You can see that they're perfect, but no one else does.

You're spending hours and hours researching companies, crafting cover letters, and reshaping your resume to align with the needs of the companies you're targeting. You toss these masterpieces downfield and hear nothing in return, as if your well-thought-out application is flying directly into a black hole.

Shakespeare writes of Unrequited Love, where the hero longs for an out-of-reach partner who doesn't respond. In your job search, you're experiencing Unrequited Job Interest.

You are desperately interested in a job, but you're not getting anything in return. And unlike Shakespeare's Romeo, you may never woo the object of your affection into loving you back.

As a job seeker, you send your heart out hundreds of times, often with no reply, and you're expected to just deal with it. It's truly maddening, perhaps more so than romance.

Like all humans, you need validation from others. This is not a weakness, but a universal drive. When you don't receive this validation, you begin to question your credentials. If the lack of validation continues unchecked, you may draw the inaccurate conclusion that you're not worthy of what you seek, that the universe is telling you to give up, that there is a reason for all this silence. This is the uninvited impact that Unrequited Job Interest can have on you.

> **Come up with your own metric of success.**

If you rely solely on getting callbacks as the determining factor of your success, you're giving away control of your days. Instead, come up with other metrics: rate your success by the number of applications you send out in a day (which needn't be more than 2 or 3 good quality apps) or by finding at least 1 outstanding job opportunity every time you sit down to do your research. Build your own yardstick.

> **Routinely reward your hard work.**

Job searching is a marathon of daily sprints. Remember to take some victory laps. Each time you meet a metric you set for yourself, enjoy a reward. The rewards don't have to be big, just frequent and healthy. Instead of gorging on an ice cream cone, hitting a bar, or binge-watching Netflix, drink tea with a friend, go for a walk, or allow yourself to read a good book. A reward designates the successful conclusion of something. It's a great way to transition out of job-search mode and back into your regular life.

> **Track your progress.**

You can't have any sense of accomplishment if you don't know what you've done. Whether a spreadsheet, a mobile app, or Post-it Notes on your wall, be sure to track your applications from the start. Job searches can take 3-6 months or longer. It won't be long before you're unable to remember all the places to which you applied.

You can geek out on this part of your job search as much or as little as you want to. There are several commercial products and subscription services out there. If you choose to build your own tool, be sure to include the company, what excited you most about the job, the date of the application, the dates of your follow-up correspondence, and some space for notes. I'd suggest creating a separate tool for interview tracking.

> **Optimize your email.**

Make sure you use a professional-sounding email address. Consider creating a brand-new alias dedicated to your job search. That way, you can set up filters to organize your correspondence and ensure nothing vital goes into your spam folder.

> **Follow the rules!**

You won't get through if you don't play by the rules. Follow the application instructions exactly as they're written, even if they sound ridiculous. Rejection is much more tragic if you're a great fit but you gave away your shot because your application was never reviewed.

CHAPTER 3

Job Boards
A Beacon of Nope

It's easy to stand in the crowd,
but it takes courage to stand alone.

MAHATMA GANDHI

How Job Boards Are Messing with Your Mind

If the application process is a black hole, then job boards are like a neon yellow flashing arrow pointing to the center of that black hole. They are siren calls for Unrequited Job Interest. The likelihood you'll get a callback is slim. Worse, you may get a callback for a job you don't even want, one that undervalues you and causes you to question your own worth.

Job boards are the easiest and most popular method of looking for work, which means they're also the most competitive place to look for work and, therefore, the least likely place that you're going to find work. By far.

Somewhere between 2%-3% of jobs are filled through job boards.

It's the last resort for employers, and yet most people spend hours at a time trolling through job listings, casting a net far and wide alongside hundreds of other amateur fishermen with their eye on the same shimmering catch.

Furthermore, if job boards are your primary or only channel of applying for jobs, then you're not getting a diversified sample of feedback. As a result, you're more likely to believe what you hear, from whoever actually calls you back, even if they've got the wrong idea about you and they're just trying to fit you in a box.

The fruitlessness of job boards erodes at your confidence and lures you away from your core values in looking for work. You may start to think you've been looking in the wrong place. You'll question how much you know, what you have to offer, and whether or not you're worth an employer's time.

It happens to the best of us.

> **Diversify your search.**

You should definitely put your resume up on job boards and set up some ticklers to alert you to good job listings coming down the pike, but don't troll the boards for hours on end.

Job boards should be a small component of your multi-faceted attack. Set a timer and spend no more than 30-45 minutes/day with a small collection of 3-5 job boards.

Use other methods of discovering job opportunities, such as (tele)conferences, meetups (virtual or otherwise), volunteering, industry associations and listservs, coffee chats, LinkedIn (see chapter 9), other social media, community forums, Q&A boards, company websites, industry media, mainstream press, alumni networks, new trainings, professor/teacher recommendations, third-party recruiters (see chapter 8), and placement specialists to name a few.

Most importantly, be sure to structure your day with offline activities to balance out the thumb-intensive trolling and scrolling.

> **Spy before you buy.**

When you see an opportunity on a job board, hold off on applying, particularly if you're super interested in it.

Do some research. Google the company. Scour their website. Find recent press on them outside of their website. Check out what employees are saying on Glassdoor. Discover what the company is proud of and what they're struggling with.

Then, see if you can find out who's doing the hiring and stalk them on the Internet and social media. Go a little deeper and see if the excitement endures.

> **Apply to the company directly.**

Even if job boards turn up an opportunity, don't apply through them, since you'll be placing yourself alongside thousands of other applicants.

Instead, go to the company's website and see if you can find the job opportunity there. Better yet, network your way to an employee or alumnus of the company via LinkedIn or through your own circle of friends. Use your diligent research to make a high-quality introduction and butter up your influential new contact.

CHAPTER 4

Job Listings
In the Shadow of Unicorns and Purple Squirrels

The din of the voices inside

whisper that I am a fraud, and that the jig is up.

Surely, someone will rise up from the audience

and say out loud that not only am I not funny and helpful,

but I'm annoying, and a phony.

ANNE LAMOTT

Job listings are designed to make you feel inadequate. They describe the ideal candidate, a person who likely doesn't exist. Indeed, recruiters—who spend their days trying to find these walking-talking demigods—created a name for them: the purple squirrel. Like unicorns, purple squirrels are a lovely image that doesn't exist.

There is a reason hiring managers model a job listing after the elusive purple squirrel, beyond just hoping to find one. An ideal job listing serves hiring managers well in the salary negotiation phase since they can point to qualifications that you're missing and offer less money. They also minimize the chances of lawsuits.

So, job descriptions work for the employer. What does it do for you?

Reviewing job descriptions is like binge-watching a YouTube channel of top-achieving Bodybuilders and Brainiacs. The ideal becomes the average. When you look down at your own regular self, instead of feeling pumped up, you become rundown. In comparing yourself to the purple squirrels, you slip from achieving to aspirational.

As a result, you may refrain from applying to some of these jobs and when you do follow through on applying, you're likely to be lukewarm on your self-image.

> **Remember that no one is a squirrel.**

It's so easy to think everyone else is more qualified than you, yet other candidates are probably scratching their heads at the job requirements as well. Recognize that purple squirrels are extremely rare and even if there is one out there, the likelihood they'll be found, available, and affordable is statistically pretty low. So, even if you're not checking all the boxes on the job listing but you're excited about the position, apply anyway!

> **Note the order of things.**

With job listings, the most important and non-negotiable stuff is at the top. Pay attention to the top 3-4 items under Job Duties and Requirements. If you don't have these skills or attributes, reconsider applying. However, if you've got all of the things at the top, but are missing some toward the bottom, don't get too discouraged. Apply anyway, and apply with vigor.

> **Ingest the keywords.**

Job listings are a keyword goldmine. The employer is giving you the answers to the test. Take the time to soak them up.

The words used in job listings should become part of your lexicon. You can quickly create a master list of the jargon in your industry by reviewing 3-4 job listings and writing down all the keywords; there are usually about 10-20 per listing. You'll notice that there is a lot of overlap across all of the listings. This is a good thing.

Here's a trick a lot of resume writers use: if you really want to geek out on keywords, drop the content of 5-10 target job listings into a "word cloud" tool to get a visual diagram showcasing which keywords are most frequently used and, therefore, most vital for you to ingest into your presentation, on paper and in person.

> **Address the hidden requirement.**

Don't just read what's written; look at how it's written. This will give you a window into the culture of the organization. Are they snarky? Corporate? Casual? Creative? Hyperbolic? Warm?

Mirror this mood in your correspondence with the company. In hiring, attitude trumps nearly everything else. Attitude denotes culture fit and all companies prioritize keeping their beloved culture intact. As a former recruiter, I'm here to say you can beat out a purple squirrel if you go in with the right attitude.

CHAPTER 5

Resumes
Tweaking the Mona Lisa

While adding the finishing touches to a painting

might appear insignificant,

it is much harder to do than one might suppose.

CLAUDE MONET

How Resume Editing Is Messing with Your Mind

Can you imagine trying to convince an artist to redo her paintings for each person that walked into the gallery? What if we told a journalist to rewrite his blog post according to who visits his website? Ludicrous! Yet, this is exactly what's expected of us as job seekers.

Resumes are masterpieces. They're self-portraits of your best side. An exquisite work of art. And they take just about as long to create as any of da Vinci's achievements.

But, unlike the great Mona Lisa, resumes are never finished. You are constantly tweaking your resume, or at least you're supposed to be, each time you apply for a new position.

It's another brick in the road of the one-sided uphill climb that goes with any job search: you're told to keep changing yourself. This is not healthy. No one wants to date or work with a chameleon.

Every time you tweak your resume, you're chipping away a piece of yourself and filling it with a different piece. In time, you'll stray so far from the original masterpiece that you'll be staring at an ambiguous rockpile. Tweak your resume enough times and in enough directions, and you'll break your spirit.

Following are some quick ways to edit your resume so you can avoid recreating the Mona Lisa every time you see a job you like.

> **Change the first three words.**

The only content you should incessantly change on your resume is the first few words, which should be a position title that lines up with the target job at hand.

If your title is Program Manager and the job you're applying for is Senior Project Manager, consider changing the former to the latter. A word of caution: look out for super-unique job titles. For example, if a company is advertising for a Head of Anti-Chaos Engineering, just go with Operations Manager. You want to look like a great fit, not like someone who is trying desperately to look like a great fit.

> **Don't rewrite. Reshuffle.**

Instead of rewriting everything, focus on shifting whole sections around, placing the most relevant stuff higher on the page.

Reorder the bullet points in each job, restack the keywords in your competencies list, change the sequence of your technical skills, and reprioritize the bullets in your summary section, if you have one. This way, you'll be catering your content to the job description without losing your story (and yourself!) in the process.

> **Slash your job titles.**

Keyword bots are smart. They know where to find job titles on a resume. To thwart the bots, feel free to give yourself 2 or even 3 keyword-rich job titles, separated by a forward slash. For example, let's say you're a Marketing Coordinator but you want a job that focuses on market research. You might use "Marketing Coordinator / Market Research Analyst" as your new title. If asked about it in the interview, say that you included your actual job title as well as your functional job title that better explains what you do. This slash technique works great for LinkedIn profiles as well.

> **Change your style.**

This one is optional, but often overlooked.

Color matters, particularly if you're applying to your dream company. You can find the RGB and HEX color palettes of public companies by doing a quick web search. Only change the color of your name, headings, and/or job titles. Don't use more than 2 colors.

> **Hire a pro from the get-go.**

The best professional resume writers will create a resume that's easily "update-able," meaning, you'll be able to tailor your resume for a job listing in 2 minutes or less.

CHAPTER 6

Cover Letters
So Many Introductions, So Little Time

First impressions can work wonders.

J.K. ROWLING

How Cover Letters Are Messing with Your Mind

You're at a party or on an app and every single person wants to meet you and they all want you to be the most interesting person they've ever met. Oh, and they're only giving you a few seconds to make your introduction. Ready... go!

Tweaking the resume is tedious enough. Now you have to recreate yet another document that just reiterates your skills all over again. Is this really necessary?

Yes, cover letters are still a thing.

Not all hiring folks want to see them but some do, which means you have to create one for each job opportunity. The unfortunate thing here is that, unlike your resume, this masterpiece may never get read. Still, you have to obsess over it like another work of art, lest your hiring manager might swipe left on you.

You are, of course, interesting but it gets tiring figuring out how to be interesting to everybody, particularly through writing. And it's even more disillusioning when you consider that your audience— the employer—is "meeting" a bunch more people before and after you, each with the same goal of being the most interesting.

It's daunting. The problem is if you're bored writing yet another cover letter, people are going to be bored reading it.

> **Create a short, non-cheesy lead-in.**

Consider kicking off the letter with a direct, short, conversational statement that illustrates your value proposition clearly. For example, "I make sure projects finish on time" or "Data is my life" or "Companies that think ahead come out ahead." Distilling your essence like this will help you focus and will wake your reader from their stupor.

> **Keep it brief.**

Good news! Cover letters have gotten shorter, probably because hiring managers' attention spans and the allotted time to search for candidates have shrunk as well.

In your first paragraph, mention your years of experience in the industry and in the role, making sure it lines up with what they're looking for. Then, have 3-5 bullet points that address the salient duties and requirements on the target job description. You want to show you're qualified point-for-point. Conclude with a thank-you and the usual "I look forward to meeting you" comment.

Even with the brief cover letter format, you should personalize it for each job, adding an intro paragraph that talks about why you're interested in the company and the role.

> **Explain away something sticky.**

Create a longer letter if you need to explain something in your work history.

For example, if you have 2 or 3 careers running in parallel, show how they fit together. If you have a job outside of your dominant career, share how it's relevant. If you're making a career transition, explain why you're well equipped to do so. If you have an unusual work history, make the case why it makes you an even better candidate.

You can't do these things with a resume, in its limited format. That's why the cover letter is a golden opportunity to bring these things in to the discussion. Don't wait for the employer to mention this stuff. Instead, get the conversation started now, in your own flattering words, and then finish it up in the interview.

> **Include a postscript.**

P.S. stands for "postscript" and postscripts always get read. People are just too curious.

Good content for a postscript includes a short testimonial from a supervisor, a quote you love, your own succinct work philosophy, explanation for a nickname you have, a special project you completed, a bizarre accolade or award, a fun fact about yourself, or a "congrats" on recent press about the target company.

CHAPTER 7

Networking
You Shmooze, You Lose

Sometimes, people are put off by the whole business of
networking as something tainted by flattery
and the pursuit of selfish advantage.
But virtue in obscurity is rewarded only in Heaven.
To succeed in this world, you have to be known to people.

CHIEF JUSTICE SONIA SOTOMAYOR

How Networking Is Messing with Your Mind

The number one way to get a job is to know someone. This undisputed little statistic is the birthplace of Networking — the mechanism we use to become someone who knows someone. The value of networking is so pervasive and universally accepted that entire industries have sprouted up around it. Tons of organizations have networking at the heart of their business model, including social media sites, executive matching firms, and conference centers.

Yet, almost no one likes networking, especially in person. And very few people like networkers.

It doesn't matter how good the pitch is or how intriguing the branding statement is (e.g., "I make regular people like you into millionaires overnight!"), you know when it's happening to you and it never feels good. You may be listening in self-interest or out of curiosity or even out of envy, but not because you actually feel an affinity with this person.

A real connection is impossible through a shtick. Deep down, you know this to be true, which is why you hate networking.

Networking puts you back in the "seller" mindset, which is uncomfortable for most of us. Networking also tends to make us feel needy and insecure (e.g., "I'm so desperate for work, I'm begging strangers for a job"). And for those introverts out there, networking is often considered an actual living hell. Don't believe me? Just ask the person hovering over the punchbowl.

The bottom line is you definitely should be networking, but how do you get to a place where you actually want to take part in this required job-search ritual?

> **Ditch the pitch.**

Canned responses suck. People would rather hear you fumble around in an authentic way, than deliver polished prefab answers to their questions.

I'm sure you'd agree that the best wedding vows and commencement speeches are unscripted and involve stuttering, crying, and mistakes. That's because awkwardness denotes vulnerability and vulnerability is what makes us feel closer to one another.

> **Talk about something else.**

Your counterpart is more likely to remember your hot tub story than your branding statement. Remember, you're just trying to make a genuine connection; it doesn't have to be about your brand or your product.

Instead, try talking about your breakfast, your vacation, your kids, your entrepreneurial struggles... Speak from the heart. My fail-safe opener for networking is to ask someone how their morning went. It gives me a window into the person's life in the here and now. They don't see it coming, so they give a real answer. And we're off in the right direction.

> **Give to get.**

A golden rule of effective networking is "Give to Get."

It feels good to be of service and people reciprocate generosity instinctively. So, think about how you can help this person. Tell them about an article you just read, a podcast they should check out, a friend who had a similar problem, a book you heard about.

Become a resource and watch the business cards and text messages come flying. They may not offer you a job in that moment, but when you reach out to them, they'll respond. That's what networking is all about. The "Give to Get" strategy works extremely well for LinkedIn, too. More on this later.

> **Network with people you know.**

It doesn't always have to be with strangers. A sad truth is that we rarely talk about our careers with friends and family, aside from venting and complaining. If you're like most people, your friends barely know what you do, or how well you do it. It's time to make a phone date and change that.

Remember, no elevator pitches. Explain a project you loved working on, share your origin story. And invite them to share theirs. Make new connections with old contacts.

CHAPTER 8

Interviewing
Dancing Naked
for Complete Strangers

Naked in front of strangers?

I can barely stand naked in front of my lovers,

in front of myself.

CLARA OSWALD

My graduate professor wrote a book on interviewing titled Dancing Naked *because that's what it feels like when you're trying to impress people who are firing questions at you like they're shooting bullets at your feet.*

Dancing naked in private is fine, indeed, therapeutic! But dancing naked in front of strangers, well... it's literally the stuff nightmares are made of.

Most people see interviewing as a power game in which the hiring manager and her mighty inquisition team have all the power and hold all the cards. They stand between you and your own prosperity, with that "What are you gonna do for me?" look on their faces and a six-shooter full of hollow-tipped "gotcha" questions.

Very few folks actually look forward to interviewing, but the ones who do are extremely successful. You can be that person.

> **Remember your power.**

We often forget that the person on the other side of the table is hoping to find you as much as you're hoping to find them.

As a former recruiter, I can tell you hiring managers want the job search to end. ASAP. They're banking on you—their next interviewee—to make that happen. That's your power.

And here's some more power: no matter how incredible you think this job is, there are more jobs out there that are equal to it or better. The math is in your favor. They need you just as much, if not more, than you need them.

> **Interview them back.**

The interview is a two-way street.

Instead of dancing naked, ask some questions yourself. Go into the interview with an agenda: 3-4 points you are going to make regardless of their questions. This agenda will ground you. It's your home base. You'll never blank out since you'll always have something to go back to.

Rather than sitting there thinking "I hope they pick me," flip it around. Think "Is this company good enough for me? How can they help me?"

And, at the end of the interview, use the following question to find out how you did, *before* you leave the interview. Ask "What character traits make a person successful in this role?" They will proceed to tell you exactly what they want to see in a candidate and you can check your work to fill in any blank spots you may not have covered yet. It works like a charm and you leave feeling like a million dollars.

> Lead with enthusiasm, and boatloads of it.

The interview is not the time for your poker face. Let your passion flag fly. Make sure you're genuinely stoked about the opportunity on at least 4 levels: the industry, the company, the culture, and the role. And be ready to share this excitement, whether they ask you about these things or not.

If you're feeling like you're faking your way into excitement, then admit that this job is not for you, and not worth your valuable time. Or theirs.

> Accept that you may never know why.

There are tons of reasons why companies say NO, most of which have nothing to do with you. They may have an inside hire, they may have lost the budget, they may have pivoted in a new direction, they may have changed management.

Definitely ask for feedback, but realize it is not in the company's best interest to give it to you. They risk litigation. So, don't push it. Accept it. Be gracious. And move on.

CHAPTER 9

Recruiters
Kneeling Before the Gatekeepers

You may not control all the events that happen to you,

but you can decide not to be reduced by them.

MAYA ANGELOU

You can see the golden city in the distance — a jeweled and sparkling land where promise and opportunity abound. Alas, the city is gated and the elusive gatekeeper flitters past the doorway, twirling the keys around his finger, seemingly uninterested in you and the line of visitors behind you, clutching at their packs.

Talk about power! Recruiters, much like castle guards, have all the keys. They have all the jobs, but for some reason, they don't seem to have all that much time for job seekers.

You end up feeling like an outsider, no matter how darned qualified you know yourself to be. Recruiter feedback can be cryptic and blunt, which can leave you questioning your credentials. Everyone seems to know more than you do. Everyone's talking to each other about you but, somehow, you're not in the conversation.

> **Don't hate the player, hate the game.**

Here's what's behind the recruiter hustle: the less time a recruiter takes to fill a position, the more money they make.

Most recruiters are contingency recruiters, aka third-party recruiters; they work for the company, not for you. Nothing personal. It's the company who is handing them a 20% commission check against your salary.

You, of course, have the option of hiring a Retained Search Firm where you pay the recruiter yourself, but most job seekers prefer not to invest tens of thousands of dollars in a job search, especially while they're not working. So, be happy you're getting a free service, however truncated or rushed it may be.

> **Talk to many, not one.**

Just as recruiters work with many job seekers at once, you should work with several recruiters. Set up a network of search/placement specialists to increase your odds and equalize the power dynamic. And don't limit yourself to working with local search firms. A recruiter may recruit for the New York market but live in Palm Springs for the lifestyle.

> **Use a broker.**

If you're looking to get in front of a ton of recruiters overnight, consider working with a resume-writing firm. Several resume writers offer Resume Distribution Services that deliver your resume to hundreds, even thousands, of recruiters with the click of a button. Recruiters value strong resumes — they seek out professional resume writers because they know they'll be able to impress their portfolio of companies.

> Know what you want.

Recruiters will respect you immensely if you come to them clear on what you have to offer and what you can do for their companies. And when they respect you, they're more likely to hook you up, so have your story straight.

> Digest the hard feedback.

In the lonely expanse of nonresponsiveness during your job search, feedback is food. And recruiter feedback is filet mignon. Be humble and gracious, even with the harshest of critics. Rejection is hard, but if a recruiter takes the time to tell you why you didn't make the cut, it means they think you're worth it in the long run.

CHAPTER 10

LinkedIn
Your Life Story on a Billboard in Times Square

Above all,

be the heroine of your life.

NORA EPHRON

How LinkedIn Is Messing with Your Mind

Writing your life story is hard enough, but when you know for a fact that hundreds of people are going to be evaluating your story in a public forum, it gets even more ominous. Everybody's watching!

To add more weight to the challenge, you are forced to write a single profile for yourself, regardless of how many interests, careers, aspirations, and job searches you have going on.

Human beings are complex. The most interesting and qualified people have twists and turns in their work histories, nuances to their roles, fortuitous mistakes, and usually more than one persona they present to the world. LinkedIn requires that all of these complexities collapse into one neatly organized value proposition.

This is a daunting task. Trying to distill yourself into a monolithic job candidate can leave you feeling one-dimensional, incomplete, exposed, misrepresented, or even dishonest — not the best headspace to be in for your job search!

Further, you may not like the idea of "bragging" about yourself and your accomplishments. The notion of tooting your own horn goes against your grain, and doing it in a public forum makes playing that song all the more uncomfortable.

> **Pick your voice.**

Before you even start writing, do this exercise: on a scale of 1 to 10 with 1 being start-up casual and 10 being corporate professional, write down the number that designates how you want to be perceived. Consider your industry, your role, and your region when making this selection.

Once you commit to a single voice, you'll feel more focused in terms of *how* you want to write. From here, you can move on to *what* you're going to write.

> **Use the summary to your advantage.**

The summary section is an open-ended invitation to say whatever you want. Use this to your advantage. Yes, you should stuff tons of keywords into your summary, but also take the opportunity to explain the trickier things in your work history.

The LinkedIn summary is a rare opportunity in the job-search process to get a bit personal. Unless you're an industry luminary who "needs no introduction", take a moment to let people know who you really are.

> **Use your resume as a guide.**

Do your resume first. If you're in a hurry, just cut-and-paste sections of your resume into your profile. That can tide you over for a while. When you have more time, try to summarize things a bit and match your Experience and Education sections with your chosen "voice." As a general rule, your LinkedIn profile should be shorter, more personal, and more modest than your resume.

Having your resume and LinkedIn profile aligned will leave you feeling whole, which will boost your self-confidence and self-efficacy.

> **Have your allies chime in.**

Once you've told your story, invite your colleagues to validate it. With LinkedIn, you can do this via recommendations and endorsements. Remember the "Give to Get" rule of networking? Use it with LinkedIn: give someone else a recommendation and they'll most likely reciprocate.

> **Show your image.**

A picture is worth a thousand words. Make sure you have a good, close-up profile pic that is not too polished but not too casual. And change your background image from the default design to something that reveals your interests, location, and/or aspirations.

Remember Your OOFS

The Job Search makes us crazy because we get stuck in our head having both sides of an imaginary conversation that no one else knows about. We come up with our own unproven reasons why we're not hearing back from employers, and it's often about our shortcomings. Within a few weeks of not getting a response, we feel isolated, ignored, and disempowered.

The key to overcoming this is to remember your OOFS – a formula you can follow that will diversify your efforts and leave you feeling accomplished every day.

Online

This one is easy. This tends to be our default with the job search: us and our laptop scrolling through job listings and social media. That's cool. There are great resources online. You should be online. Just not all the time.

Offline

This one is harder, but no less important. In fact, it's more important. You have to get away from the scrolling and trolling. The only way you're going to find the other side of a conversation is by being in front of someone else. You have to get out of your head.

To break free, set up lunch dates, coffee breaks, walk calls, informational interviews, meetups, group chats, virtual hot tub hangouts, whatever. Attend conferences, association meetings, webinars, church, and wherever else your people are. Share where you're at, get another perspective, find referrals, and make opportunities.

Getting "out" and offline doesn't mean you have to go outside. Think of it as getting out of your head, not necessarily your home. You need a shift in perspective, the possibility of something new. That's what's important.

Follow-up

A sense of accomplishment is only possible with some reflection, and follow-up work helps you remember what you just did. It can include thank-you notes, confirmation calls/emails, check-ins, pick-me-ups and resources for other people, and of course, follow-up on applications. Following up on things is what prevents you from feeling like you're running in place and helps you to feel like you're working toward something.

Self-Care

If you're not in good shape, mentally and physically, you're not going to produce good results. You already know the healthy things you like to do. Do them. Give them to yourself as a daily reward. Recognize the truth that you're not merely taking a break. Rather, you're keeping your sanity and refueling yourself with the energy that your job search will inevitably take away. No matter how hard things get, always remember: it's not you, it's your job search.

QUICK REFERENCE

Personal Branding
- Don't sell yourself. *Show* yourself.
- Test your story to remember your greatness.
- Trade your elevator pitch for an IM intro.
- You are not a product

Job Applications
- Come up with your own metric of success.
- Routinely reward your hard work.
- Track your progress.
- Optimize your email.
- Follow the rules!

Job Boards
- Diversify your search.
- Spy before you buy.
- Apply to the company directly.

Job Listings
- Remember that no one is a squirrel.
- Note the order of things.
- Ingest the keywords.
- Address the hidden requirement.

Resumes
- Change the first three words.
- Don't rewrite. Reshuffle.
- Slash your job titles.
- Change your style.
- Hire a pro from the get-go.

Cover Letters

- Create a short, non-cheesy lead-in.
- Keep it brief.
- Explain away something sticky.
- Include a postscript.

Networking

- Ditch the pitch.
- Talk about something else.
- Give to get.
- Network with people you know.

Interviewing

- Remember your power.
- Interview them back.
- Lead with enthusiasm, and boatloads of it.
- Accept that you may never know why.

Recruiters

- Don't hate the player, hate the game.
- Talk to many, not one.
- Use a broker.
- Know what you want.
- Digest the hard feedback.

LinkedIn

- Pick your voice.
- Use the summary to your advantage.
- Use your resume as a guide.
- Have your allies chime in.
- Show your image.

RESOURCES

*Stay connected, conscientious, and confident,
and great things will happen for you.*

*Your story is wonderful, in all its inevitable imperfection, struggle,
and triumph; the kind of story worth reading about,
featuring a hero(ine) worth hiring.*

Like our style?

Read more career advice articles:
https://advice.brightsideresumes.com/

Get personalized help:
https://brightsideresumes.com/

How Are You Feeling Now?

Take a moment. Anything different?

If you found any of this advice helpful, if you found yourself nodding along or enjoying an a-ha moment or two, please consider sharing your experience with other readers.

As you know, reviews are what make people choose books. If you think your fellow job seekers should choose this one, take a minute and click on some stars to help them with their decision.

If not, that's cool. We'll win you over with the next one.

Thanks for reading. Stay bright.

Made in the USA
Las Vegas, NV
10 June 2021

24432645R00046